D0860159

POWERED UP!

A STEM Approach to Energy Sources

WIND FARMS

Harnessing the Power of Wind

THERESA MORLOCK

PowerKiDS press

New York

Published in 2018 by The Rosen Publishing Group, Inc.
29 East 21st Street, New York, NY 10010

Copyright © 2018 by The Rosen Publishing Group, Inc.

All rights reserved. No part of this book may be reproduced in any form without permission in writing from the publisher, except by a reviewer.

First Edition

Editor: Melissa Raé Shofner
Book Design: Tanya Dellaccio

Photo Credits: Cover XXLPhoto/Shutterstock.com; p. 5 Angela Rohde/Shutterstock.com; p. 6 WDG Photo/Shutterstock.com; p. 7 (palm trees) Jim Lopes/Shutterstock.com; p. 7 (waves) Benny Marty/Shutterstock.com; p. 9 (windmill) jorisvo/Shutterstock.com; p. 9 (windmill interior) Hivaka/Shutterstock.com; p. 11 (Palm Springs wind turbines) Francois LE DIASCORN/Gamma-Rapho/Getty Images; p. 11 (Charles F. Brush) https://commons.wikimedia.org/wiki/File:Charles_F._Brush_ca1920.jpg; p. 11 (first wind turbine) https://commons.wikimedia.org/wiki/File:Wind_turbine_1888_Charles_Brush.jpg; p. 12 (horizontal-axis wind turbine) Ron Zmiri/Shutterstock.com; p. 12 (vertical-axis wind turbine) Joseph Sohm/Shutterstock.com; p. 15 kamilpetran/Shutterstock.com; p. 16 Skylynx/Shutterstock.com; pp. 17 (wind turbine assembly), 20 (London Array project) Bloomberg/Getty Images; p. 17 (wind turbine construction) Sean Gallup/Getty Images News/Getty Images; p. 19 (top) The Asahi Shimbun/Getty Images; p. 19 (bottom) https://commons.wikimedia.org/wiki/File:Secretary_Kerry_Holds_Granddaughter_Dobbs-Higginson_on_Lap_While_Signing_COP21_Climate_Change_Agreement_at_UN_General_Assembly_Hall_in_New_York_(26512345421).jpg; p. 20 (wind farm in Copenhagen) Yann Arthus-Bertrand/Getty Images; p. 21 DON EMMERT/AFP/Getty Images; p. 22 Jesus Keller/Shutterstock.com.

Cataloging-in-Publication Data

Names: Morlock, Theresa.
Title: Wind farms: harnessing the power of wind / Theresa Morlock.
Description: New York : PowerKids Press, 2018. | Series: Powered up! a STEM approach to energy sources | Includes index.
Identifiers: ISBN 9781538328552 (pbk.) | ISBN 9781508164241 (library bound) | ISBN 9781538328613 (6 pack) real
Subjects: LCSH: Wind power-Juvenile literature. | Wind power plants-Juvenile literature. | Power resources-Juvenile literature. | Clean energy industries-Juvenile literature.
Classification: LCC TJ820.M8417 2018 | DDC 333.9'2-dc23

Manufactured in China

CPSIA Compliance Information: Batch #BW18PK For Further Information contact Rosen Publishing, New York, New York at 1-800-237-9932

CONTENTS

ENERGY IS EVERYTHING

What is energy? Why do we need it? Where does it come from? Energy is the power people use to get things done. We need energy to run machinery and produce heat and electricity. People harness Earth's **resources** to generate, or create, energy.

The wind is one of our greatest energy resources. People have used wind power in different forms for thousands of years. As **technology** continues to advance, wind energy is becoming cheaper and more useful than ever before.

SUPERCHARGED!

The world's population increases each day. More people means a greater need for energy. A few of Earth's other energy sources include the sun, heat from within our planet, and moving water, such as ocean waves.

WIND FARMS ARE AREAS OF LAND WHERE WIND IS HARNESSED TO PRODUCE ENERGY.

WHAT'S WIND?

Wind is naturally created by conditions in Earth's **atmosphere**. The sun heats Earth's surface unevenly. When land heats up, the hot air rises and cool air moves down to take its place. This moving air creates wind.

Many things affect wind speed. For example, moving water carries hot air away quickly. That means areas with water are usually windier. Wind near the ground moves slowly because it has to move around trees and other land features. That means wind high above the ground moves much faster.

SUPERCHARGED!

Strong wind currents can be found between 6 and 9 miles (9.7 and 14.5 km) above Earth. These currents are called jet streams. Jet streams can blow at speeds of more than 250 miles (402.3 km) per hour!

WIND IS AIR IN MOTION. WIND CHANGES EVERY DAY BASED ON THE WEATHER, BUT SOME WIND PATTERNS, SUCH AS JET STREAMS, HAVE BEEN **IDENTIFIED.**

WIND POWER IN THE PAST

About 5,000 years ago, ancient Egyptians began using wind to sail their boats up the Nile River. Between AD 500 and 900, people in Persia (modern-day Iran) used wind to help them pump water and grind, or crush, grain. Later, around AD 1000, Europeans began using wind power to drain lakes.

Boat sails were the first known way to harness wind power. Later, windmills were developed. A windmill has sails (also called blades) that are turned by the wind. As the sails turn, so do gears inside the mill.

SUPERCHARGED!

How does a windmill grind grain? When a windmill's sails turn, they turn large, circular stones called millstones inside the body of the mill. The millstones grind grain, turning it into flour.

IN THE NETHERLANDS, WINDMILLS—SUCH AS THE ONES PICTURED HERE IN KINDERDIJK—ARE A COMMON SIGHT.

INSIDE OF A WINDMILL THAT GRINDS GRAIN

ADVANCES IN WIND POWER

Over time, several advancements were made to existing windmill technology. In 1888, the first electricity-generating wind **turbine** was invented in Cleveland, Ohio. This turbine used 144 wooden blades to generate electricity. In 1890, steel blades were invented for windmills and turbines. Steel replaced the older wooden blades and cloth sails, making windmills more **efficient**.

In 1973, an oil shortage created a greater need for **alternative** energy sources. In the early 1980s, the first large wind farms were established in California. The wind power industry was on the rise.

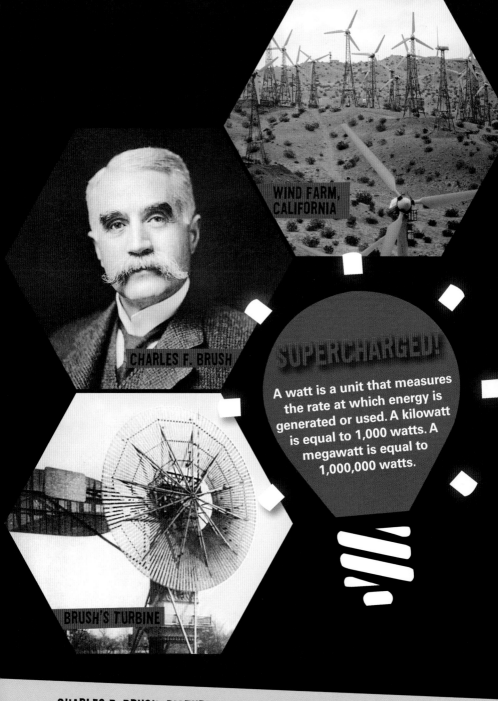

WIND FARM, CALIFORNIA

CHARLES F. BRUSH

BRUSH'S TURBINE

SUPERCHARGED!

A watt is a unit that measures the rate at which energy is generated or used. A kilowatt is equal to 1,000 watts. A megawatt is equal to 1,000,000 watts.

CHARLES F. BRUSH, PICTURED HERE, WAS THE CREATOR OF THE FIRST ELECTRICITY–GENERATING WIND TURBINE. HIS TURBINE STOOD 60 FEET (18.3 M) HIGH AND GENERATED 12 KILOWATTS OF ELECTRICITY.

HOW IT WORKS

A simple wind turbine has two or three blades. The blades are connected to a spinning piece called a rotor. The rotor is connected to a **generator**, which sits on top of the main part of the turbine, which is called the shaft. When the wind blows, the blades turn. The spinning blades cause the generator to spin, which creates electricity.

In some kinds of wind turbines, the **axis** is horizontal, or in line with the ground. In other kinds, the axis is vertical.

HORIZONTAL-AXIS TURBINE

VERTICAL-AXIS TURBINE

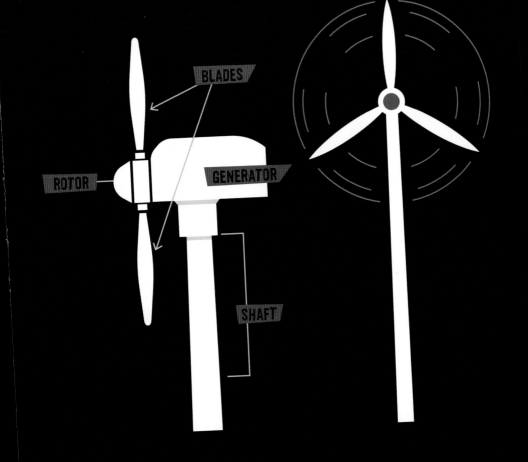

BLADES

ROTOR

GENERATOR

SHAFT

THERE ARE TWO BASIC TYPES OF WIND TURBINES: HORIZONTAL-AXIS AND VERTICAL-AXIS. HORIZONTAL-AXIS TURBINES ARE MUCH MORE COMMONLY USED THAN VERTICAL-AXIS TURBINES.

SUPERCHARGED!

Wind power is a form of kinetic energy. Kinetic energy is the energy of motion.

13

NONRENEWABLE VERSUS RENEWABLE

Wind is a renewable resource. Many energy resources, such as fossil fuels, are nonrenewable. Nonrenewable means that once they're used up, they're gone forever.

The most popular energy sources are fossil fuels. Unfortunately, burning fossil fuels produces **greenhouse gases**, which trap heat close to Earth's surface. This is known as global warming. Fossil fuels are also running out. Scientists are looking for more ways to use renewable resources, such as wind power.

SUPERCHARGED!

Fossil fuels are fuels that form inside the earth from dead plants and animals. This process takes millions of years. Fossil fuels form too slowly to be considered renewable.

BURNING FOSSIL FUELS, SUCH AS COAL, OIL, AND NATURAL GAS, CREATES A LOT OF POLLUTION. WIND POWER IS MUCH BETTER FOR THE ENVIRONMENT.

THE WONDERS OF WIND

There are many benefits that come with using wind power as an energy source. Wind energy is clean. That means that, unlike fossil fuels, it doesn't pollute the air. Wind energy is also cost effective. Wind turbines are much less expensive than other energy technologies. Plus, the process of building turbines creates jobs.

Wind energy is a domestic resource. That means it's readily available within the United States. Also, wind turbines don't take up much space and can be built on empty land.

SUPERCHARGED!

Some people object to wind turbines because they think they're too noisy. That's a small price to pay for the many benefits of wind power!

SCIENTISTS BELIEVE WIND POWER CAN REDUCE GREENHOUSE GAS **EMISSIONS** BY 14 PERCENT BY THE YEAR 2050.

WHO USES WIND POWER?

Wind power is used throughout the world. In 2012, Iceland became the 100th country to use wind power. Today, eight countries lead the production of wind power: France, Canada, the United Kingdom, Spain, India, Germany, the United States, and China. China is currently the top wind-power producer. The United States is the second largest.

Altogether, the wind turbines in the United States have the power to generate 74,471 megawatts of electricity. In Iowa, 31 percent of the state's power comes from the wind!

SUPERCHARGED!

China generates about one-third of the wind power of the entire world. China's turbines have the power to generate 145,362 megawatts of electricity.

WIND FARM,
WAKKANAI, JAPAN

ON APRIL 22, 2016, THE UNITED NATIONS CREATED AN INTERNATIONAL AGREEMENT TO REDUCE GREENHOUSE GAS EMISSIONS. FORMER SECRETARY OF STATE JOHN KERRY IS PICTURED HERE SIGNING THE AGREEMENT FOR THE UNITED STATES.

OFFSHORE TURBINES

Wind turbines are often built on land, but some are built in the ocean! Winds that blow over the ocean are more powerful than winds inland. Offshore turbines are able to produce a lot more energy.

The first offshore wind turbines were built in 1991 off the coast of Denmark. Most offshore wind farms that exist today are located in shallow waters around Europe. The United States has just recently begun work on an offshore wind farm near Long Island, New York.

COPENHAGEN, DENMARK

LONDON ARRAY

IN 2016, BLOCK ISLAND WIND FARM, PICTURED HERE OFF THE COAST OF RHODE ISLAND, BECAME THE FIRST OFFSHORE WIND FARM TO OPERATE IN THE UNITED STATES.

SUPERCHARGED!

The London Array, located off the coast of England, is the largest offshore wind farm in the world. It has 175 turbines!

THE FUTURE OF WIND POWER

Over the past decade, the use of wind turbines has increased by more than 25 percent each year. In the United States, over 53,000 wind turbines currently stand in 41 states and Puerto Rico and Guam. These turbines have the ability to power about 25 million homes each year.

According to the *Wind Vision Report* released by the U.S. Department of Energy in 2015, it's possible that wind energy will make up 35 percent of America's energy resources by the year 2050.

GLOSSARY

alternative: Something that can be chosen instead of something else.

atmosphere: The mixture of gases that surround a planet.

axis: A straight line around which an object turns.

efficient: Capable of producing desired results without wasting materials, time, or energy.

emission: A substance put out into the air.

environment: The conditions that surround a living thing and affect the way it lives.

generator: A machine that turns energy into electricity.

greenhouse gases: Gases in the atmosphere that trap energy from the sun.

identify: To tell what something is.

resource: A usable supply of something.

technology: A method that uses science to solve problems and the tools used to solve those problems.

turbine: An engine with blades that are caused to spin by pressure from water, steam, or air.

INDEX

WEBSITES

Due to the changing nature of Internet links, PowerKids Press has
developed an online list of websites related to the subject of this book.
This site is updated regularly. Please use this link to access the list:
www.powerkidslinks.com/pu/wind

3 1125 01086 0995